# Places Where We Have Lived Forever

## Poems by Eileen Hennessy
## Art by Ann Gillen

The inhabitants are natives and have lived there forever. I am the only stranger.

I have lived there all my life and should have left long ago but couldn't.

Richard Hugo, *The Triggering Town*

# Contents

6 **Dedication**

**I**
8 **Gone-by news**
9 **We arrived this morning**

**II**
12 **Story**
13 **Working with splash**
14 **Uncanny**
15 **Lights, out**
16 **What arrives**
17 **Happy company**
18 **The speech of birds**
19 **Departure of the Ark**
20 **Memorial Day**
21 **Wheeling**
22 **Visitation**
23 **The Conquest of Mexico**
24 **Eclipse**

**III**

26 **The exciting democracy of the news**

27 **The Big Top**

28 **A man of parts**

29 **Landscape with car**

30 **The Leader**

31 **Easter**

32 **The year we lost Magna Carta**

33 **Bitter-ended**

34 **On message**

**IV**

36 **Not. As. In.**

37 **Toy**

38 **Silence was golden**

**V**

40 **Green skies are what we aren't**

41 **What's the truth**

42 **There's confusion in the land, but**

43 **The world around us fails to disappear**

45 Appendix

# Dedication

To every village its drawn-out road,
salted down and slick as sunlight
greased to slide between the fields.
To every field its gracious sky,
its dauntless witted souls at work.
To every man his washstand, soap,
and towel, his wife with fresh hot
water for his rinse. To every house
its dog with warring tongue,
its walls and carpets clotted
with cabbage roses, its host
of drawn embroidered linens.
Its supper table
with moss and wrack, edible
in layered sheaves, bowls, spoons,
folded hands, heads bowed in thanks,
the wheel and drone of prayer.
Its drier where the children spin.
Its tumbrel in the driveway.

## Gone-by news

First, the death of God, the one
with the upper-case name. Old,
still alive when his feet trod
his primeval waters, he held on until
a bit of land came by, grew firm.
Fish drew near, tested the ground,
climbed on. Became animals.
Land became Earth, the animals roamed,
one stood on its hind legs, another,
the two gave birth
to others who stood. Then
two forked animals who spoke. The Word:
apple, choice. The world went still.

# We arrived this morning

to find the waterbugs
drunk on our desks. Such an end.
And with the high tide approaching,
bucking the in-city wind.
Will the most memorable moments

take place in our office?
We're used to *comfortable* news,
given to us in groups of two or three
gathered around the printer
in the name of

girls, or sons waiting to replace
the boss moving full steam ahead
into the sunset. Where is he
now that we need him? He knows
about infinity-edge water

overrunning the earth decor. All
we know is rain-dome showers,
the fear of the ebb tide that carries souls
out and across. Is *that* any way
to promote a tide? even one
that's world-class high.

# Story

Mingled and entwined, tall grasses blow together like eels
heaped writhing and indistinguishable in their watery
beds. Grass has little chance of achieving a successful
life story when it is grown on rooftops. Eels die young
in water that is pregnant with bacteria and microbes.
Eels are thus suitable for use in early-warning tests of the
wholesomeness of the water supply, but their stories are
often cut short because the hospitals put eels into drinks
to cure alcoholics and make their cast-off skins into garters
that doctors prescribe to ward off cramps. Otherwise, even
though once upon a time grass was offered to conquerors
in acknowledgment of defeat, it will not now grow on
the graves of criminals or innocent persons wrongfully
executed.  Their life stories flow best when written in rapid
floating lines, making it impossible to tell where one begins
so that the other can end.

# Working with splash

The river and the falls are on the edge of town, very close to the lab where I work on the project for the installation of mirrors, mist, and artificial sun-lights along the riverfront.

In the lab, believing is seeing, and righteousness is about correct branding. If I discover a belief and don't label it correctly, I can't install it. Just because a belief was discovered in a lab doesn't mean the lights last forever and the mirrors don't need to be cleaned.

Usually the riverfront skyline is solid and full. But during the summer months the water roils and the rain clouds tumble and blast a path into the Global Positioning System. Working so close to the falls, naturally we worry about the skyline. These are the months when we punch a hole in the lab ceiling, put up a ladder, and climb up to check the world outside. But it's all splatter and splash in the mist and mirrors. If there's nothing there to be believed, is there something there to be seen?

# Uncanny

The way the same things show up over and over for counting. Always deeply practical. Always impeccably polite.

On summer nights, we gather in the square to hear numbers beamed out and objects called up for the count.

Dry quiet things are the most popular because they are easier to count up or down than are moist moving things.

There is no summer night without its count of the cars roaming in the commuter parking lot, the shadows of ships quietly moving offshore.

Counting brings to life our groves of still white trees, our acorns in the park, our sparrows nibbling on droppings under the outdoor restaurant tables. Everything is so open out here. In fact, calls for head counts go out over the public address system. Sooner or later enough heads that the counting of crosses can begin.

## Lights, out

We short wide double-jobbers hold quiet dry things that like to be counted in pecks. That is, when we're filled. When we're empty, we swallow light. The world would rather we swallowed fire.

What everyone loves is the tall slim jobbers, proud and loud in their edge-hard glamour. *They* get to hold the red wine, the hops, the monkeys, the gallons on a roll. Light doesn't enter their minds.

Empty, turned upside down, we roof over spaces where the light from outside and the light from within you meet and are quenched. The best-loved haven on any city block. It's dark and quiet and you can see if there's anything else inside you.

The world is suspicious of things that like to hide from the light, and darkness knows that darkness is the place where the world begins.

## What arrives

Despite the existence of cement and a flight tax, millions of big beautiful families with frosted heads travel from city to city in municipal population exchanges, studying nudes and their nestling habits.

Smoking, we lounge in building doorways and wait to see what will arrive and how: usually by tunnel, now that the bridge that brought divers over the river to various mating places has disappeared.

At night we're at home and hungry and heavy on the sofa.

Sound of someone kicking the Welcome mat from the door.

Our excuse for not moving already a long time ago now clear.

# Happy company

Winter comes and then we wait in the well-loved front room, warmed and lighted by the sunshine that streams through the window, crosses the floor, and stops at the back-room door.

We watch and wait for the cat, king and key for us.

The cat too loves the sunny front room, the warmth, and all of us there for him. He leaps onto the wooden chair, reaches across the table, and swats the silver thimble. The thimble topples, falls, and rolls into the shadows in the back room. The scissors twitch at the swipe of his paw aimed at a broken-handled cup. The gilded picture frame on the table waits its turn.

Now the cat stands on the table, allowing a paw, his tail, then his whiskers to be framed and reframed. A black-and-white-marbled notebook remains impassive.

The winter light fades early. The glass doorknob sends flashes around the room. We watch and wait. Finally the wall clock pronounces judgment: a striking that is and is and is, louder and darker even than the motor of the king.

# The speech of birds

In winter the streets fill with the voices of shipwrecked sailors windblown to shore and lured to movie houses where they hang their dog tags on pegs when they arrive.

The moving pictures fill the blackness with long murmurs and sudden romantic or dramatic clicks that bob and connect at the end.

The sailors' dreams are short and soft. Whether we have already heard or almost heard or never heard them, we keep count in the town ledger.

We treat dreams as we treat any other cold-water creature: Put out a salt lick to keep them coming. The theory is that if we plant serpents' teeth in our gardens an army of serpents will spring up, defend us; if we drink their blood we will never die, if we cut off their heads we will understand the speech of birds.

# Departure of the Ark

At midnight it was still chewing quietly on its anchor chain while the puddles meandering along the waterfront engulfed the chunks of watermelon we'd thrown overboard after our farewell.

At two a.m., sound of the waterfront tugs suddenly flapping and churning.

In no time: us roaring out through the roads, ready for the open sea. The noise gave us all a case of the vapors. The fluids boiled in our brains. Just when we had finally relaxed into thinking about nothing worse than chipped beef!

The moon took on a distracted, uncomfortable look. The sky was ripe with reflections. Not yet visible, the jagged edge of the earth, out there where the ocean becomes a flume of falling water.

## Memorial Day

Throngs of blowfish-shaped women. Tufts of feathery hair, round-bellied men who park their trucks around the main square, and a big-haired ginger cat that attends to tittering birds. Blooms of sunshine tumble through the treetops. The sunlight has been here for years. Under the close-fitting sky, thoughts flit among the houses. Fat mice jump from step to step down front stoops. The cat goes into crouch and creep, springs. Crunch of bird-bones fine as feather shafts. The children not heard, not seen.

## Wheeling

According to this method, the children are taken out of their homes and are wound on a perpetually rotating upright wheel. The children have back-to-front story lines and primate eyes, and they have a long way to go in enormous haste. Luckily the wheel rises into the sky above the town, and its velocity is right. Resonating with its rickety sounds, the children rock through the spinning skyworld and have meetings with clouds. By the time the whistle sounds, the way has become shorter. The wheel sloughs the children off onto a rack and begins pulling up the next batch.

# Visitation

To be a tourist means to hunt new routes to any fast
land where there are tears on the buttercups. The
Barbarians knew the best places of the age: Rome, Vienna,
Constantinople. What's exotic now? Bridges bolted to the
air. Sunrise in the hills of the head. The Mermaid Inn, a
room that smells of damp heroines, the innkeeper's wife a
woman of excellent succulence. Her son, first and best of
breed, leads a group of tourists in a one-day downpour.

# The Conquest of Mexico

The guards at the building sites go on eating their lunch. The jaguars go on waiting in line to give blood. The concrete mixers go on mixing the blood into the cement for the mortar. Protesters wait their chance to paint graffiti on the walls. The building contractors go on shooing away the hungry leeches that try to fasten onto the jaguars before they reach the blood-drawing station. The wind grows stronger as it sweeps up the screams of the jaguars and the curses of the contractors and the shouts of the foreigners and carries them along the streets. After a time the foreigners stop shouting and sheath their swords and gather around the interpreter La Malinche as she explains the mortar-mixing technique. There is no interpreter to speak for the jaguars. "But we're the suppliers who provide the blood," the jaguars complain. The protesters start to spray-paint graffiti on the walls. The guards look up for a moment, then go back to their tortillas. The foreigners keep their hands on their hilts and strain to understand La Malinche, who speaks their language with a heavy accent. The jaguars go on waiting their turn to give. The leeches roll their numerous eyes and practice moving their jaws and their teeth.

# Eclipse

I did not have to count the moon-years gone by since the beginning of my time to know that what hung in the sky that night was a water-ruled seed moon caught on the shoals of the clouds, its face in darkness for a while and in light for a while and warm with the fever of spring, so that the darkness was only partly supported. That small at its starting, upward-pointing, it nevertheless kept the waters from spilling over its edge onto the trees waiting to catch it and hold it secure. That a frustrated bird could launch a thousand moons off the flight deck of its tongue. That the moons would fly up and fan out over the sky, marking it. That I would wake up to watch the spilt moonlight spread its seeds of darkness.

# The exciting democracy of the news

Despite the pain of badly bruised heels, the two men were able to improve their performance with a leap of only fifty-seven feet in whatever direction was decided by the toss of a coin.

That's one way to capture a sliver of lawn stuck with wickets to trip up invaders.

Questions were raised in our media. What was one of them doing sticking his hand into the back waistband of his shiny black shorts? What was the other one doing coming up from behind and fumbling at the waistband to help the first one do whatever it was needed doing? What was the first one doing in such a rush to move forward that he pulled the second one along with him?

Noble, these two? Not by the looks of them.

Nubile? That's a word for young women.

So what were they then? Anatomies of democracy? No, that's Greek, not Roman.

What then? How to treat them?

We argued these questions among ourselves. And in our one newspaper that publishes in private and public tongues.

The toss of a coin decided: We have no court of last resort. The decision was: It's the age of the image now. We want the paradise that's been shown to us: under the bridge, shaded from the sun glaring on the river, our last two orphan boys breaking their bread together.

# The Big Top

He's king and lord of the stays and struts that hold it all up. Okay, his glory is old and needs to be freshened, but half a halo is better than none. The people who look at things through his eyes know he's the one who keeps the top spinning. The good thing is that his roadkill keeps food on our plates during the winter when there's no work and storms cut the power lines down to more manageable heights. If the power and the glory are his, what's left? What we need is a story we can take along when we go past the caution-falling-rock sign and the cliffs to the right of us and the hard places to the left of us and on along the rain-slicked road into the roughened terrain where the hindmost gets overtaken. What we get is the bits of pieces that fall to the floor when his table is cleared.

# A man of parts

And his pin-striped shirt and silky tie and dark fine-wool suit, his shined shoes, his fedora brushed and blown, his briefcase full of case files. And so thus was he fully warped and woofed, man of presence and parts, his body spindle-wound and ready for the day to unspool it.

And the snowy Belfast linen napkin he tucked (at lunch in the restaurant next to the reflecting pool with fountainous Nereids playing at dance) into the collar around his goose-fleshed neck that rose to be gripped by his head.

And the gold family-crest ring that caught a beam of chandelier light as he dipped his fingers into the fresh-water pond in the crystal finger bowl.

Later, his shoes dimmed with the day's dust, faint wrinkles in his trousers, sulky shirt blousing above his belt, his full polished briefcase, his fedora ready to be tipped to ladies and clergymen.

Still later his dinner, the moonlight glowing on the terrace, the nightly bowl of milk for the unreflective cat, its unbearable thirst as it drank.

# Landscape with car

He picked himself up and brushed off his coat. After all, things could be made to last. He still had the peacocks and the dogs. He also got a house and a yard with a parking space. He was heaped in with the deal.

There was no sign warning that parts of the yard were unsupported. The birds piped wrong signals into the house. Over time, he found himself burdened with predictably regressed nestlings that had to be swept out.

Then the car arrived: Came spinning at high speed and crashed into the yard. And already defaced: A poorly punctuated, strongly worded message was sprayed on it in big red letters.

He did not comment or take a punctuation test. He had never been great with surprises.

# The Leader

Wasteland man come out of exile, on the day of his accession to power he announced to his people, "Your country is my country. Now go and bring me things."

In the background, sound of skittering birds hiding their nests, footfalls of people already beginning the search.

Those things that were found for him, he kept in his office together with the affairs of state. He liked having everything in one place within his reach and safe from snooping eyes and opening hands. His favorites were the round nightside lamp with square beige-and-white lampshade, the hairless egg resting in his shiny red plastic in-basket, a pearl-handled knife with curved blade designed to cut out fat, and a large bronze foot taken from the toppled statue of the leader he had overthrown, which he used as a wastebasket.

On the anniversary of his accession, he marched his followers through the city, their shoestrings tied together so they could move only as a group, their feet clinking as they marched to the drumbeats of his voice falling into place in the ground.

The birds in the park went silent. The bronze foot shifted position. The moon moved into his sign, and he was finally in his ascendance.

It was then that he realized his people would be better if they were shorter and fewer.

# Easter

So the group of friends and neighbors went on to larger
things: the cathedral bell tolling, the priest saying the
funeral mass, the choir chanting the Day of Wrath,
the corpse weeping through its coffin, until Saturday
afternoon, when the group gathered at the cemetery to
change the flowers, sweep, dust, and offer up a picnic lunch
on the paving stones even though the spirit had passed
beyond the cemetery and the city and the outlying houses
and the fields and was to be found flitting in and out
among the trees in the forest where blue jays dive-bombed
through the noisome wind and tore at the eyes of the cats
lying on the ground in wait for birds, mice, or any small
animal that could do duty as a meal once its moving feet
had recorded its story in the ground beneath last year's
leaves of the oak tree under which an empty coat was
sleeping after having lost or evicted its occupant, and all
the while the friends and neighbors, unknowing, roistered
until sunset amid the whorls of dust whipped by the wind
through the nookish shadows between the tombs, then
dragged themselves to the evening memorial service, their
muscles limp, their hands feeling for their bones, their eyes
unable to determine how much loss was still left on this
earth.

# The year we lost Magna Carta

The year we lost Magna Carta was a year of coming
down sad to breakfast every day. Between our domestic
denunciations and our tectonic faults, we continually
mistook each other for a jumble of snapshots. We made
search after search, in sallies and counter-sallies with
raiding parties; you, pretty in your wallpaper-patterned
jacket, defected early on. We took long sleeps in foundering
towns where police and thieves engaged in private wars.
In despair, we made a search for the drafts of the charter.
Filled in a blank with its name, clicked on Temporary
Documents, and selected Search by Date, Title, Subject.
Only later did we realize that it had probably been
renamed to fit into the abandoned streets of our small old
world inhabited by scribes blowing on the wrong end of
their pens.

## Bitter-ended

When we opened your crankcase, first we saw the back end of your life. Then the rest of your years came tumbling out.

Serves you right for not storing them in the stock box.

Your site was gold. So hot. So then. Right where successful neighborhoods have always wanted to be.

So that was your dilemma?

A good dinner and a change of laws later, you were on your way. That's how you rescued yourself from having to be saved.

As I remember, you were a person all thumbs with a ring. That the weighing-stone was missing from the ring made you all the more perfect.

So how did you do otherwise?

# On message

I move as if our planet were my comfort zone. I play the five fingers, sing the prayer of the seven holy hidden names. I am the proud possessor of old sane things. I am speaker of your peace, maker of your miracles, illuminator of your shadows, burner of your candles, knower of things you do not know about yourself. To communicate with me is to be a holy turning table. Be assured that our words are already in fortuitous cosmic connection. I offer you my friendship and greetings and high strong regards, and pray that they reach you in good time. I have seen the sword of your suffering. Be assured that I am using ancient spiritual magic to protect you. I am the person you can trust. This is the most important letter you will ever receive. Within hours of your call, I will be there. Even before then, there are many things that I will do for you. I have taken you for my own.

## Not. As. In.

Not *in, inside, within.* Not as in a bucket-pot of blackened iron that swung on a squealing hook above the hearth and cooked the family dinner. Thus not holding. Also not *on* or *onto*, as on a pine table on which plates are thudded or clinked or chinked to receive dinner ladled out of a pot on or onto them. Thus not receiving. Also not *into*, as in drop or sink or fall or slide into, in which a body folds itself in two right angles and fits itself into a wood or plastic half-bucket turned on its side and plain or padded with nubby bouclé or bumpy brocade or cold-butter leather. Thus not half-holding. Also not *onto* or *on* or *on top of*, as for a sleeping man stretched out on a bed, horizontal straight line above or on top of another straight line. Thus not bearing or supporting. Not any of these. Then what. *Is.* As in It is that it is. Standing alone, left alone, let be, letting be, counting moments from to on out.

# Toy

It was a green windup tank with bright yellow treads running like twin belts along its sides. It moved with a thin little rattling noise. It also moved very fast, for a tank. Another interesting thing was that after traveling straight ahead for a while, it would veer off suddenly at an angle. Every few seconds its hatch cover would open, and a tin soldier would pop out, as far as his waist, and look around. He was wearing a khaki uniform and helmet, and a long, fringed, white silk scarf that waved behind him in the breeze. Holding binoculars to his eyes, he scanned the room, his head moving from side to side with small jerking movements. Then he slid back into the tank, and the hatch cover closed over him. This went on until the day the cover closed down too soon, cutting off the soldier's head, which fell to the floor. The blood gushed up out of his body with such force that it blasted the hatch cover right off the tank.

# Silence was golden

Money talked. Fur bespoke wealth. Ermine said one thing, sable said another, beaver said something else again. No two of us heard the same words. We had all heard other words in the thick brown fog that ended when the city closed the mines and we picked up our settlement checks and left. The move was not easy. Moving in fur was never easy, because of its bulk. Yet we wore it all year round. Along the road my move became even more difficult when a schnauzer mistook me for a squirrel and attacked. The dog's owner was a woman in grey and a look of nothing more. Her testimony in the case fell on hard closed heads. The judgment handed down by the court ordered the taking of a powder and a dusting of the overbite. The court officers sealed the judgment with red wax and put the schnauzer on track to its ultimate destination.

# Green skies are what we aren't

sites temporarily unavailable.

Green skies are the new black—
have positive curvature wherever a lane
intersects them in hyperbola.
Blue planes are in the travel section
with aspects of contract furniture.

The latest blue planes I have seen
have big wings and long to climb
to the green-skies project
that telegraphs Hail! to tomatoes

Blue planes are spreading.
Not available in Kansas anymore.
Decent when in robot mode,
lower in the underground weather.

What's the percentage
of blue planes with input image?
They certainly won't replace
the weather-alert sirens.

What's behind green skies and stormy weather?
At each intersection there's a dark plain
where great marauding Danes strip paint.

# What's the truth

about that beautiful weather attributed to the eye?
It leaks into breeding groves for gnats.

Storms are always in the eye of the beholder.
We never lose our talent for blind turns into rain.

Mosaic eyes stare out of walls.
None of them anointable as god of sight:
that takes an adequate head, a glowing eyepiece.

The eye of God is a light flashing on an eyestalk.
When a storm meets that eye, the colors almost match.

Our gaze gets lost in the swarm of new gnats,
their long trail across our rose-tinted windows.

# There's confusion in the land, but

here's an answer:
*This momma-house (no dogs permitted)*
*is storm-tossed cloths hung on dry*
*lines between poles.* What's the question?
*When will you leave it?* Not this spring,

with your boils already blooming.
This past winter,
the authorities leveled a 300-year-old
dune left out of their promise of land.
A critical crack: shifting ground

makes for a bumpy ride, the kind of test
nothing in school can teach you. So far
at least you kids are still okay: little
hillocks of joy in a beach-grass act,
playing it safe on the lit-up sand.

Remember your test number. Because
sooner or later it's sayonara, all you kids
in your sunsuits. Whatever your grade,
you too get to hide in the ground.

# The world around us fails to disappear

Induces a condition with medical solutions
that may not be reproduced or distributed.

How to tell when we want help
redirected by a professional native?
Check the orgasms we like:
mini-league predictions that provide
backwards compatibility.

It's just like us to cause a scene,
while we eschew the hot potations,
addict ourselves to tankards of ale.

Meanwhile, our lips balm by the sea.
Spring delights shimmer and shine
on our lively hands.

# Appendix

## Note

Epigraph: quotation from Richard Hugo, *The Triggering Town*
(New York and London: W.W. Norton & Company, 1979 [1992]), p. 19

## Poems previously published

"Dedication"
Published as "United States Poem Number 5," *The Journal*, 22, no. 2 (Autumn 1998)

"Eclipse"
*Off the Coast*, Fall 2011

"Not. As. In."
*Borderlands: Texas Poetry Review*, No. 24, Spring/Summer 2005, p. 3

"The Year We Lost Magna Carta"
*Margie – The American Journal of Poetry*, Vol. 3/2004, p. 155
[Finalist in First Annual "Strong Rx Medicine" Poetry Contest, 2004;
Russell Edson, judge]

# Statement by the Poet

Ann Gillen, the sculptor, and I, Eileen Hennessy, the poet, are cousins on our mothers' side. Such a short sentence, yet one that encapsulates countless generations of known and unknown links, physical, emotional, mental, spiritual, and geographical!

Reviewing my poems, my sculptor cousin "recognized in our separate arts similar structural organization involving the aesthetic disciplines of time, energy, and movement." Her words, encapsulating a set of relationships between and among the arts. On what is that recognition based? On our shared heritage? On our respective upbringings? On a complex of other, more generally human factors too tightly interconnected to be separable, in the current state of our knowledge of our human condition?

Movement and energy: Those are, precisely, the traits that have always attracted me to Ann Gillen's work. It was only natural, then, that I turned to her when I began thinking about a book that would be a work of two arts, the visual and the verbal. What was the genesis of this concept? Simply this: it seems to me that poems written in response to visual art works represent a fairly common genre, but that nowadays fewer works of visual art are being created in response to modern and post-modern poems. I was curious to see what might result from a collaboration by two artists, verbal and visual, working in this particular human society, that of the United States of America, at this particular time in history.

This book is one result of that collaboration. Another result is the pleasure I experienced and the insights I gained in our discussions about our respective processes and works. Collaborations of this type are a remarkable learning experience, and I think the arts, and our society, would benefit greatly if they became more common.

A poet and short story writer, Eileen Hennessy's poems and short stories have been published in numerous literary journals, including *Confluence*, *The New York Quarterly*, *Paintbrush*, the *Paris Review*, *Western Humanities Review*, and others. Her collection of poems *This Country of Gale-force Winds* was published in 2011 by NYQ Books. Her translations of art history books, chiefly from French, include monographs of various modern artists, a history of esthetic theory in the Middle Ages, and books on the representation of European cities in paintings. She translates commercial and legal documentation into English from French, Italian, Portuguese, Spanish, Dutch, and German. An adjunct associate professor in the translation studies program at New York University, she teaches courses in French-to-English legal translation in the Certificate and Master's programs. She holds an M.A. from New York University and an M.F.A. from Fairleigh Dickinson University.

## Statement by the Artist

Eileen Hennessy, the poet and I, the sculptor, are cousins on our mothers' side. Our grandfather was an artist who worked for the Fredrick Keppel & Co. Gallery that carried Whistler's prints when they were new. His daughter, my mother, was a painter. Reviewing my cousin's poems I recognized in our separate arts similar structural organization involving the aesthetic disciplines of time, energy, and movement.

Our joining of word with image was simple because of this insight and mutual respect. My prints are the visual energy of the poetry. I drew many figures of the poet charging across the page. She is the large figure, the dominating poet, moving through her environment in her isolated world. Her suggested movement is what is important; she is stripped of detail as is the environment. This use of any background is unusual in my work.

The figure, the human body, is a symbol that regenerates with significant meaning in each historic era. For me the human body must unite with motion. Not in the passive Renaissance body-mind connection but as the actively charged dynamic figure claiming the world through physical action.

Eileen Hennessy has ordered the poems so that there is a path to follow in the reading. My prints are inserted at the beginning of each section. At that juncture the rhythm of the book changes; the eyes stop reading the straight lines of the text. There is a print. The images are looked at across the page and from up and down. This new reading rhythm refreshes the eyes and the reading mind. It reactivates the tempo of the book while leading the reader on to the next section. The bold cover is to entice a new reader to come and begin the reading journey.

Ann Gillen constructs sculpture in various materials. Besides fabricating personal work she has completed 30 commissions; the red sculpture on the sidewalk of 3rd Ave. at 55 Street since 1989; Lincoln Center's Garage Plaza; CUNY'S School of Journalism; a New York City Percent for Art commission; the State of New Jersey; the 1980 Winter Olympics. Her earliest work, a 1958 woodcut scroll book is in the collections of the Fogg Museum at Harvard University and the Brooklyn Museum. She is in Irving Sandler's archive collection at the Getty Research Institute. Recently, the Bowdoin College Art Museum received a sheet metal study as part of the Vogel collection. Gillen has had solo exhibitions beginning at the E. Weyhe Gallery, and lastly, at R. Pardo's Galleries in Chelsea and in Milan. She has had retrospectives at Wave Hill, Vassar College, and the Stamford Museum. Group exhibitions include the Storm King Art Center and the American Academy of Arts and Letters. She is represented in the FEMINIST ART BASE of the Elizabeth Sackler Center at the Brooklyn Museum. Gillen earned a B.F.A. from Pratt Institute and a M.F.A. from the School of the Arts at Columbia University.

*Places Where We Have Lived Forever*

ISBN: 978-0-9791495-5-9

Off the Park Press
73 Fifth Avenue, Suite 8B
New York, New York 10003

Distributed by
Small Press Distribution
1341 Seventh Street
Berkeley, California 94710

800-869-7553
www.spdbooks.org
orders@spdbooks.org

Book Design by Nancy Linn